Fourteen to Fortyish: The Formative Years

Fourteen to Fortyish: The Formative Years

Poems of Love, Love-ish, and Hope

Claudia Williams

© 2015 by Claudia Williams

All rights reserved. No part of this publication may be reproduced, stored in a retrieval system, distributed, or transmitted in any form, or by any means, including photocopying, recording, or other electronic or mechanical methods now available or that may become available in the future without the prior written permission of the publisher.

For permission requests, email the publisher, at: inquiry@cawingcrowpress.com

Published by:
Cawing Crow Press LLC
Dunlo, PA

ISBN: 978-1-68264-000-5
Library of Congress Control Number: 2015951422

Visit us on the web at: www.cawingcrowpress.com

For you and me

"Lightly men talk of saying what they mean. Often when he was teaching me to write in Greek the Fox would say, "Child, to say the very thing you really mean, the whole of it, nothing more or less or other than what you really mean; that's the whole art and joy of words." A glib saying. When the time comes to you at which you will be forced at last to utter the speech which has lain at the center of your soul for years, which you have, all that time, idiot-like, been saying over and over, you'll not talk about joy of words."
- C.S. Lewis

"Love recognizes no barriers. It jumps hurdles, leaps fences, penetrates walls to arrive at its destination full of hope."
- Maya Angelou

"To love at all is to be vulnerable."
- C.S. Lewis

Contents

Acknowledgements	xv
Introduction	xvi
Inner Cogitations	1

Phase One

For the Love of Me	5
What do You See?	6
Love of My Heart	7
At Water's Edge	8
The Colour of Love	9
Insecure	10
I Can Dream	11
I Love You	12
Happy Valentine's Day	13
At First	14
To You	16
How Small I Am	17
'Til My Love	18

Fluid Movement	19
Dancing Country in White	20
Have I?	21
Always on My Mind	22

Phase Two

Remorse	25
And All the Roses	26
Now and Then	27
Dying Swan	28
Scared Heart	29
Almost the End	30
The Real Reason	31
Between the Lines	32
Oops!	33
Aftermath	34
Say When	35
Out of love	36
Break Free! – Pt .1	37
Break Free! – Pt .2 (Virgin territory)	38
Your Dream	39
Friend	40
Thoughts of You	41

And Still	42
This Was Too Good	43
Mi Heart a Hurt Mi	45
Friends First	47
I want	48
To Love and Lose	49
Life-Changing	50
The Haunting – Pt. 1	52
The Haunting – Pt. 2	55
I Miss You Hard	58
My Spot	59
I'd Rather Not	60
That Fall in Letchworth Park	61
The House Does Not Work	62
That Thing You Did With Your Toes	63
Like Dying	64
You Should Have Told Me	65
Please Call Me	66
I Called Your Mom Today	67
She Could Have Been Ours	68
Some Days I Don't Miss You	69
It's Just Not Fair	70
Shifting Moral of the Story	71

The Power of Your Words	72
Out of This World	73
Just Friends	74
I Miss That	75
Nothing That Mattered	76
Out of Time	77
Other Than Myself	78
An Image of You	79
Nothing	80
I Just Don't Feel Like It	81
A Moving Target	82
Sometimes There Are No Thoughts of You	83
The Nights Have All Been Spent	84
Without the Kill	85
Not Again	86
You Can't Make This Love Up	87

Phase Three

Open Your Eyes – and Love Me	93
I'm Always Thirsty After Poetry	94
Sand in My Shorts	95
Company	96

Bayou	97
With Every Other Step	98
Time and Company	99
Naked	100
Just for a Moment	101
How Do You Know	103
Air	104
Epiphany	105
Your Kisses	107
Requited Love	108
Closer	109
Rush of Love	110
Back to Life	111
About the Author	113

Acknowledgements

I'd like to thank God, and all the people who made this possible. No, really.

This is the good part. This is where I get to tell my parents, Irvin and Joyce Williams, that you both have been amazing in loving and supporting me. Yes, if given a choice to do this over, I'd choose you both in a heartbeat. My sisters feel the same way.

And, speaking of my sisters, Nadine, Latannia, and Durel, you think you know, but you have no idea how thankful I am for your love, and for always believing in me.

Thanks to those who read, listened, edited, and gave feedback in some way. I met Daniel Kojo Appiah, (@OZionn), an award-winning poet from Ghana, via Twitter. He was a tough but thorough beta-reader. This work is better because of him.

It was a pleasure working with Cawing Crow Press as they helped make this book a reality.

Along the journey of life and love and writing, I've had friends who've kept cheering me on. I've had strangers whose kind words kept my chin up. And, I've had "loves of my life" from whom parting was sweet sorrow - the kind that inevitably gave birth to poems.

For all, I am thankful.

Introduction

I do not have a story. I am a story. I have a voice. For many years, I have been using my voice to share myself with others. I have grown. I have loved. I have lost. And, I have learned along the way to be happy. In this anthology, I share the highs and lows of new love, of what I thought was love, of unrequited love, of loving thickly, of vulnerability, of hope, and of words — the right words. "Some day I'll find the right words — and I'll write them down," I've often told myself. Had I done that, or emailed them to myself, or tweeted them, or chiselled them in stone, or carved them in wood, I wouldn't be searching for the right words for this introduction. But, I digress. Sorta.

In sharing how I came to this place, I cannot sugar-coat the journey. It is written here as it was; as it has been so far. The poems have been written in the ink of pain, sometimes confusion, sometimes hurt, and sometimes that mix of delight and pleasure sprinkled on like Parmesan. And, occasionally, whatever that emotion is when you know it's all going downhill and you want to convince yourself you'd be fine if you hurtled after it because you want so bad not to lose it and there's nothing you can do to stop it and you're driven to sadness while bracing for the inevitable even though you know no loneliness hurts as bad as being miserable feels. Yeah. That one. My fonts of choice? Sarcasm, humour, resignation, grit, steel, some anger, a degree of longing, but mostly, care.

The sweet spots in writing these poems have been found in the highest of highs - "There's no drug like adrenaline," as ALIAS character, Sydney Bristow said -and in the lowest of lows. There's hardly ever an in-between. The journey has not been all beautiful, nor all ugly. But, it is written.

The poems are laid out in phases, and within each, in chronological order — from early teens to Fortyish. This anthology spans almost three decades. (My, when I put it like that!) I've written poems on the pages of notebooks - when I should have been paying attention in Physics class. I've recorded them on a mix tape, just for the then love of my life. I've written them on fancy stationery created using Corel Draw, just for the then love of my life. I've emailed them and SMS'd them, just for the then love of my life. I've WhatsApp'd them and BBM'd them, just for the then love of my life. I've blogged them and tweeted them — as coded messages - just for the then love of my life. And, I've written them and kept them in my journal, or in *Keep*, just for me.

I've often written that what would please me most after publishing, is for at least one person to say they can relate. Relatability. Hey, slicing my heart open does not hurt as much as having it broken. If you can relate to this, if you have loved and lost and loved and lost and loved and lost and may be wondering what it is you did or didn't do, this one's for you. Relate to this, too: Hope floats. I still believe in true love.

Sometime along the journey, I learned happiness is a choice. I could sit and mope about what I don't have, or I could count my blessings and see that I have much to be thankful for. And, I am learning to live in each moment — the gift of right now.

All I have is this moment and a choice.

- Claudia

———

The Poems

Inner Cogitations

For what reason did I come here?
For what purpose was I born?
To taste of agony and of pain
Or, to appreciate the sudden joys
That last for just a moment.

Am I here to watch and learn
From mistakes made by others?
Or to make them myself
So others can learn from mine.

Is it so hard to say, "I'm sorry"?
Too painful to touch truths
That lie within
Subconsciousness?

Facing the future with uncertainty
Which can only be outshone by
Unfailing love
Security
And peace of mind.
Relieved to know that
Someone cares.

PHASE ONE

— TOO GOOD —

For The Love of Me

When two people grow to appreciate each other
Against odds real and imagined
It is one of the most beautiful
Things that can happen
The most beautiful of all dreams come true.

Of all the people in the world
Of all the girls in the world
Of all the dreams in the world
Look at me, being appreciated by you.

What Do You See?

In that flame, I see you

And I see me

Sitting by that same flame

Saying that we see each other.

The black wick symbolizes

The hard and trying times we go through

But, there is always hope

As the blue flame shows

And, it leads up into

That pyramid of bright light

Depths of sheer peace and joy.

Love of My Heart

Beat of my heart
You play
A very great part
In me.
I guess I never really knew
How much I relied on all of you
Until I nearly lost you
Afraid to lose you
Missing your caring
My heart began to break
Soundlessly.

I tried to laugh away
Those feelings of rejection
My attempt at a happy face failed
It was directly opposite
To the appearance of my heart.
Those two contrasting features
Could not be of the same person.

I prayed...longed...hoped...waited
For another chance.
Now that I have got it
I am grateful.
I know I'm truly blessed.

At Water's Edge

Water splashes at my feet
The wind carries salty air
Across my face.
My body bathes in
Calm, cool, peaceful
Nature.
Water. Wind. Birds.
Tranquility.

Suddenly, a seagull cries
As it takes flight from shore to sky
I hear splashes and gurgles
As waves hurl themselves against rocks.
I walk toward one that's been gently kissed by mist
From this safe distance, I sit and reminisce
There was a time when I enjoyed this enchantment
With you.

The Colour of Love

The colour of love
As I see in your eyes
Is the silvery sheen of the sparkling dew
As it falls from the leaf of the orchid.

It is the red-orange of the sun
As it sinks, slowly
Setting the horizon on fire.

It is the soft, delicate pink of a rain-washed rose
Like the one you brought for me today.

It is the small starry glow
That shows in your eyes
When you smile.

But, above all
It is the bright, white light
That forms at the centre
Where our gazes meet
When you tell me you never want to lose me.

Insecure

Life is slipping away
Going.
I can't hold on to anything
Not for long, anyway.
Like trees and light posts and grass
As I stare out the small window of the train
It is slipping, slipping out of reach
Going, going, gone.

You won't leave me like that, will you?
Please, don't answer.
As skies above are pale and vague
So I think your answer will be.
At this moment, anyway.

For, we both don't know
What the future will bring
We have only hope and desire
To be together. Always.

I Can Dream

Maybe you won't hold me tight
As often as I want you to
Maybe you won't kiss my lips
My face, my neck
As I long for you to do.
Maybe you won't tell me you love me
As often as every day.
But, I can dream about
These things — and more
While you are away.

I can dream we're on
A moonlit beach
Somewhere in the dark
Or that we're taking lovely pictures
By the river, in the park.
Or, better yet, we're holding hands
Walking toward the sunset.
And we're laughing at your silly joke
Walking toward the sunset.

But these dreams are no more
Than what they are, just fantasies
That sometimes help to ease the pain
Of not tasting realities
They are things you can hold on to
Which makes them last much longer
Than realities that come and go
Making your longing stronger.

I Love You

You are a most special human being
And you make me feel special.

I love you loving me.
It thrills me all over to know
That I am loved by one so
Wonderful.

I love you wanting me.
Your desiring me
And my passions
Excites me beyond measure
I am grateful for all the pleasure
That you give.

I love you needing me
It makes me feel special
To know that you
Think my opinions
Worthwhile.
Your genuine smile
Greets me in the mornings
And I am filled with
The wonder of you all.

Happy Valentine's Day

Darling after all this time
You still excite me to the core
And although I'm with you everyday
I wish I could be with you more.
In my every dream about you
Whether it be night or day
I hope they would come true
In every possible way.
So here's to you, my darling
From a heart with love sincere,
A Happy Valentine's Day
And an even happier year!

At First

At first it didn't matter
If you cared
As long as you were there
To share
To be
With me

It didn't matter
If you thought of me as special
I already thought so
Of myself
I could hold my own
With or without you.

My heart was still
Beating to the
Rhythms of the cruel sounds
Of yester love
The lies. The tears. The unspoken fears.
I could not
And I would not
Until I chose.

And amidst the important things
And the things that didn't matter
You came.

But I would be as hard as rock.
If you decided to leave
I needed to be able
To go my way

Untouched. Unhurt.

It didn't matter — at first
If you cared
I didn't give a damn
But now, it does
And I do.

To You

To you who need me and my care
Who act as though I were not there
"What does a woman want?"
You ask.

I am a woman
By that I've said so very much
But still you ache for more.

Except that which is illegal, immoral or crazy
There is little, if anything, left
I know.
But, if that's the way it has to go
Then let me do
Whatever it is I have to do
Right.
And, while I'm at it
Do you as you have never been done
Before.

How Small I Am

How small I am to your eyes
That look upon me
And yet
Cannot surmise
The magnitude of my will
Over yours.

Your incompetence is highlighted
By your indifference

You do not have to
Measure yourself
Against me.
No need to do battle
For me.
I am already yours.

'Til My Love

My mind goes back
To when I first met you
How ordinary the meeting
But I knew I had to get you
The first time I spoke with you
The silly things I said
The first time we laughed together
The first time we shared.

The little nuances of others
About whom we had cared
The first time we held hands
And mine felt so cold
So I led you to places
More inviting.

The first time we locked fingers
And I thought, this is good
The first glimmer of hope
That lit the rest of the road.

So many things came after
So much has been the laughter
And the tears
From laughter. Mostly.

I have grown to love you
To need you needing me
And, I have come to realise
That you will never be.

Fluid Movement

When was the last time
I danced into the night?
Moved and worked my body
In molasses-like motion
And, at times, the soca wine
Doing the double thing
Unsure waves
Running back to ocean.

You danced. A little.
Then some more
Then next to me
Moving to the beat of the same Dollar
Fanning our bodies as we glowed
Hands on hips.

Workey.
Double time
Then slow.

How do we do this?
Moving slower, still
To Beres' "Black Beauty"
Never heard it before until
You sang — and did it well
The last slow dance with
Just a friend.

Dancing Country in White

You were the only one who knew
Country songs make me feel sexy
That they bring out the dancer in me
I close my eyes
I'm dressed all in white
Cropped top and wide-flowing skirt
Barefoot
On a white-sand beach.

Have I?

How can it be
I miss you so bad
The vacancy of you not being here
Though I have not met you yet.
Or, have I?

The longing for you
Hoping and yearning for your return
After you have gone away
And I have not met you yet.
Or, have I?

Always On My Mind

I came far away to see whether
I could get away from you
Four thousand miles isn't
Far enough I see.

There is no distance in feeling
In the way I long for you
The moment I landed
I began missing you.

My mind is always with me
And you are always on my mind.
How can I get away
When I don't want to get away?
When I wish, instead, to keep you
In my heart
And on my mind?

PHASE TWO
— Love's Illusions —

Remorse

I wanted to touch you
I wanted to hold you
I wanted to feel the warmth of
Your cheeks against mine.

I wanted to tell you how much
I longed to let you know
That I feel for you.
That I want you here.

My heart aches in trying
To let you know I feel remorse.
Guilty of burning my bridges behind me.
If only I could reach for you now.
If only.

And All the Roses

He spoke to her harshly
As she walked through the door
And all the time they'd spent together
Didn't seem to matter anymore.

It had been a long time
They knew each other well.
But, somehow, things were not the same
Anybody could tell.

She loved him dearly to her heart
And he, her, to his soul.
But he had betrayed her trust
And her love had grown quite cold.

He had planted a garden of roses
To soothe his burning guilt
She loved to watch him tend the plants
As he covered their roots with silt.

Then the roses began to fade
And she, feeling ill at ease
Asked him if anything was wrong
He said he could do as he pleased.

The wind blows even colder now
It whistles loudly inside
Weeds have taken over the garden
And, all the roses have died.

Now and Then

I think of you now as we were today
Reliving the past in the present.
We say the same words
We have the same expressions
And I capture it all for a moment.

The smiles are the same
As are the actions.
Even the jokes you tell.
But, as I reminisce, I sigh.

For now, I think different thoughts
For those sentiments you shared
Your words that excited and pleased me
And, instead of acting cold and indifferent
Now, we are together. Alone.

Dying Swan

Here I am all alone.
By choice.
By my stupid, punishing, frustrating choice
I cling to every hint of reason
That tells me I'm in the right
And desperately try to find
That great redeemer.
That tells me this makes sense

If I were brave, I'd say, "Return."
"Return," I'd plead, "to me with love.
The love that caused you to hate and hurt
With the passion meant for the lover."
These arms and lips they yearn for you.
The dying swan's first song is almost through.

Scared Heart

He chants the rhythms and I am held
Suspended in time and Bandele's face
"Let me belong to me
Before I belong to you."
Each beat sets my heart nearer breaking.

My heart's afraid of breaking
So it will never dance.
My heart's afraid of breaking
It will never take the chance.

He sings of you. He sings of me.
Though — God forbid — he knows it not.
Our problems, highly universal
Yet belonging only to us

We nourish them with insecurities
'Til they inflate — then burst like a sore.

My heart's afraid of breaking
So it will never dance.
My heart's afraid of breaking
It will never take the chance.

Almost the End

He left me bare
Stripped me of my pride
Took my peace of mind, Stole my soul
Left me to wander aimlessly
In a world of guilt and pain.

He played with my emotions
Toyed with my sense of being
And now I've lost trace of who I am
Who I ever dreamt of becoming.

Like a new-born child to the universe
I'm helpless, innocent, and curious
Like Cupid in his work shed
I know the whats, the whys, and hows.

He left me bare,
Stripped me of my pride,
Left me feeling so very strange
With my love sealed inside.

The Real Reason

Then, he was gone.
For always.
The strange thing is
He was not missed
And, he was not mine
Anymore.

It was not because of any one person
But, rather because of
People
Things and
Places.

Stones. Blocks. Wasps. Birds. Bees .
Nature? Sure.
And pigs fly.
He thinks I don't but
I do know why...

Between the Lines

I sit looking through the pages
And I know that
I'm not seeing
That which I'm supposed to see.
I'm not seeing the words
I'm not seeing you
With me.

Oops!

I was sure I saw it
In your eyes
I heard it in your laughs
I saw it in your smiles
I couldn't have mistaken it
For anything but love
I was so very sure of it
I could have put my life on it
It was pure and free and just enough.

Your actions were bilingual
For your words were few
You didn't say what I wanted to hear
But, I knew you had it in you.

Now, you have come and touched and gone.
And your impression was so deep.
The prints, erased
But scars remain,
And tears fall
Like spring rain.

And, I may just fall for you again.
I know me.

Aftermath

As each came
I poured and poured
Out of the reservoir of my being
My heart, will and emotions.
Just a little at a time
Until, finally
I was emptied
Drained.
The last drop.
I was left tired and weak.

Then I slipped from me
And broke!
And sent sounds echoing through my mind
Rather, the pieces of my mind
No peace of mind
My cries unheard
In silent, falling tears.

Say When

As with an unborn child
It is easier for me
To let my fantasies
And dreams about us
Remain
Untouched.
Having given birth to them
I cannot push them back
From whence they came
And, it would be a hard
And callous thing
To kill them.

So, then, let them be.
Whether or not I choose
To reach out and
Bring them here
Totally depends
On you.

Out of Love

I have always heard that one
Should find oneself in love
I never knew that oneself
Could be found out of love.

I have always asked
Who am I?
Never realizing that
I could find out so much more
If I had asked
Who am I not?

Maybe this is how it goes:
You know you are in love
Yet, on feeling rejection
You "decide" that you
Might not have had a
Self-inspection. Realization.
I didn't know I was like *this*!
Finding out things about yourself
You had not thought you were.
Finding yourself
Out of love.

Break Free! – Pt. 1

This body of mine has a spirit
This heart of mine has a soul.

Break out, pressed heart!
Set free yourself, chained spirit
Let your wings take you
To places yet unknown
Virgin land, yet to be spoilt
By feet that think they know
So much about so much.

For every drop of tear that falls
An ounce of strength within you grows
And you have been cryin'
For a long time.

So break out, strong heart!
Piece yourself together
And let your spirit fly
Fly!
Fly high
Unto peaceful, virgin territory.

Break Free! – Pt. 2 (Virgin Territory)

Recently, all my thoughts of you
Have flowed from tears
Salty, burning, irritating water
That springs from a bleeding heart.

Why do you cause me so much pain?
I thought by now I'd have refrained
From wishing to be near you
Desiring with every nerve and sinew
To be loved by you again.

Cause me joy, cause me laughter
Cause me to be happy ever after
You tell me that you have to go
I feel empty without you, so
I'm going to wallow in this
My pity of self.
Weep and sob until the knob
Of the door is turned
Inviting me
Into peaceful, virgin territory.

Your Dream

Can I... borrow your dream?
It's funny but it seems
Yours is so much brighter
Filled with more — more hope
Mine, on the other hand, is laced
With inhibition, doubts and longstanding
Evidence — caused by a misunderstanding —
That it will not be realized.

So, before I lose
All faith in my future
May I borrow yours for a minute?
While I try to suture
My edges which I've all but gone over
It's like crimson and clover
Or black and white
No shades of pink or grey
You either have one or you don't
Dare you lend me your dream?
I'll either return it — or I won't.

Friend

Just a little at a time
I'll get there
Where?
Crazy! Out of my mind!

You do not want me
You just want me to want you
Then you take me
As you want to.

After so long, I'll learn
I must
Give myself time to rest
To ease this pain within
I want to hate you
For not loving me
But I can't
Because now
You're a friend.

Thoughts of You

Let me steal
Just one thought of you
It's my dream. I do as I please.
I decide whether or not to touch you
Whether to kiss you
I decide whether
You decide to touch me, hold me
Kiss me.

Passionately you execute
All your movements
All our sensations fettered
On each our strong desires.

While I'm away from you
Not knowing whether
You still care about me
Or, if you do
Whether you still want me
While I try to imagine being held
By someone else. Anyone else.

While I try not to confess to myself
That which my heart has long ago realized
While I try to forget that
I'll always remember you

Let me steal
Just one more thought of you.

And Still

"If you can wait
And not be tired by waiting."

I have spent
Almost a third of my years waiting
For you
You who have now found
Someone new.

I saw it coming
I knew it would hit
I just didn't know
That the blow
Would be
So low.

Now, I don't know
And yet, I know
So much
But, I don't give a damn!

And still I lie.

This Was Too Good

We held hands and formed
A small circle of something special.
I've played this happy tune
One too many times
Here I go again.
I have turned my back
On he who made me laugh
He made me comfortable
He made me happy
This had to be good.

Do you know what it's like
To feel your dreams
Die within you?
Washing each with a tear
Before laying it to rest

Each flame of hope that you kindled
Burns low
Then, with no breath of desire
To fan its cheek
It slowly dies.

Do you know what it's like
To return to your fantasies
Having to face the harsh reality
That there'll be no more of
"Those times."

You came like a fresh breath of spring
And, to my life you brought

Your laughter
The fulfillment of my dreams
Seemed you brought
Everything.

Now the leaves are turning brown
And, like my spirit,
Falling.

Some people touch
And then they're gone
How many more times
Am I going to have to say
Goodbye.

Mi Heart a Hurt Mi

Six night ago mi lose mi love
A felt wi simply had to part
But tonight mi hear sopm a splinta
When mi look good, nuh mi heart!

Mi nuh know how mi a go manage
Him was mi star in di velvet sky
Now him gone right out a mi life
An all him whispa was goodbye.

Dem seh fi "tek kin teet kibba heart bun"
But "bad luck wuss dan obeah"
For how mi a go in love wid him
If wi nuh inna it togedda?

Everyting remine mi a him
From familia cologne to a shoe
An mi dis lef fi shed eye wata
If mi si a Subaru.

Mi know seh him nuh know seh
Mi still love him bad cyaan dun
An mi deh ya a tink seh
Mi nah go have so much fun.

For everyting we did was good
Some tings betta dan di res
An in di back a mi head mi a tink
How we a go buil we likkle nes.

But, a gooda dat frighten him yah
Him won't even talk him mind
Mi mussa love him into a state a shock
Him probly never meet one a mi kind.

Di fact of di matter is dat
Mi want him back til mi short
Mi already bawl blood, sweat and tears
A now feeling an attack a di heart.

Di long an short of it is
Mi want him nut him nah know
'Cause mi definitely nah tell him
And him not here to see it show.

Any which part yuh deh mi love
Mi mine constantly deh pon yuh
Which is why mi cyaan fine it of later
Oonu come back to mi. Du!

Friends First

I long so much to hold you
To gently touch your face
To sit with you and just be
And feel your warm embrace.

My mind is working overtime
To find a way to say
Everything that is in my heart
But I just can't find a way.

We talk and laugh together
We really do have fun
Yet, it seems it's not enough
My thoughts are on the run.

I'm thinking I like you more than a friend
Too late to stop that now
So when you ask to be friends first
I have no idea how

To think of you and not glow inside
To see you and not touch
May time bring you back to me
I want you oh so much.

I Want

I want to wake up one morning
Knowing that I won't be calling you
Knowing that I won't be seeing you
Knowing that I won't be loving you.

I will wake up that morning
And go through the day
        And go through the evening
                And go through the night.

                        And, the next morning?

I would have
        gone through the day before
                Without you.

                    And, the next morning?
I would have
        gone through the day before
                Without you.
                    And so on.
                          And so on.
                              So, there.

To Love and Lose

If you take yourself away from me
I will be okay. I promise.
But you would have to do it now.
One day more
And I would have tipped the scale
From okay to aching
And a remake of that longing
I had before you came.

Go ahead and go
Before you stay here longer
And stain the beauty of
My memory
With the futility of desire.
Time sometimes wounds all heals
Go before I remember
What it feels like
To love and lose
Again.

Life-changing

I am waiting on a new heart
This one seems to be worn
There is no feeling
I should have felt
Something
When your words
Sliced through it today
Swift. Clean. Bloodless.
Which heart has time to bleed
When it's busy going numb
When it's busy dying.

I am waiting on a new tongue
This one seems to have lost its taste
It has got used to saying
I love you
Wanting to kiss you
One long kiss
Yesterday. Today. Tomorrow.
But, I could only imagine
And day dream
At night.

I am waiting on a new you
You seem to have gone
Your space is here
But your place is
Elsewhere
Just the way you like it
Right?
Comfort zone. Alone.

If the formula works
Don't change it
Right?
Ah, Ruthie.

I am waiting on new air
Mine is all used up
I'm stifling.
Not allowed freedom
To weep or die
Too much hope.
Not enough pain.
Who would have time to die
With a new heart, and tongue,
And you.

The Haunting – Pt. 1

They say I must situate myself in my Thirty-something.
It's The Haunting.
It has to be.
The feeling that I'm waiting on my life to start beyond Thirty-something.
Call it now, Close-to-Forty.
For that is nearer truth.
That is truth, actually.

The feeling cripples me.
Makes me want to go out and do things.
Things I know I can do
But won't do
For The Haunting takes over.
Too late, it says. Too
Late.

Too too late.
So, why start?
And I get lost
In the lie.
It is a lie
But, it's now familiar.

The familiar, Haunting
Darkness
Overwhelming no.

That haunting, familiar, lie and no
Has become
Comfortable.

Almost home
But not.

It's comfortable not to move.
It's comfortable to under-achieve
While always seeming to overreach —What was that about o'er-leaping ambition?

I don't want this to be my home.
I do not want to live here.
Get me something else that is not familiar,
Not so familiar.
(No one will hand it to me.)

I will get me something else
That is
The unfamiliar

I can't
But
Succeed.

Me.
Succeed
Beyond my wildest and most vivid imagination.

I mightn't recognize the Me I'll come to be
But,
I'll be out of the reach of
The Haunting.
I'll be out of the reach of voices that pretend to wrap me in
comfort,
But whisper only lies;

And out of their reach
I'll fly
Thirty-something, maybe even
Close-to-Forty
Light years
High.

The Haunting – Pt. 2

It's The Haunting
You know.
You have to reach down
Down
Deep down
Deeper still...
There...
No...
Deeper yet
Just a little more
Then
Aah!

That's it.
That's where honesty
Lies
Comfortably.
The truth that only you know
Beyond all doubt.
This is what you know in your heart
To be so.

No one else knows.

Truth is hidden
Truth is ugly
Truth is

I'm scared to death!

I'm so afraid of failing
At that which
I believe I would do best.
That which could not be done by any other
As well as it could be done by me.
It is only mine to do
It is unique to me.

It's The Haunting.
It has to be.

How could I possibly fail
At that which is uniquely mine to do?
I don't know how —
I just can't seem to get past
That I will.

And, what is more
I don't want it bad enough.
I need to want it
Bad
Enough.

I want to want it bad
My want has to become
Something stronger —
A need.

A need to want it like I want nothing else.
A need to want it like
It's the only thing I've ever wanted in my life.
The only thing I want to do with my life.
The only thing that is my life.

Begin to believe
That I can reach down,
Way down past
The twice-defeated
The honesty
And The Haunting
And the truth
That now is.

Touch a tri-mass of
Love and life and laughter.
Inspire me.

My fingertips have touched it.
I'm wrapping my hands around it.
I'm holding tightly to it
Squeezing the life out of it;
Squeezing my life out of it.

And I find myself
Where I want to be.
Home.

I Miss You Hard

I want to cry but the tears won't come
I knit my brows trying to prompt them

Nothing.

I miss you hard.
As hard as it is to admit to myself
That I want you.
As hard as it is to swallow this truth.
I wish you were here.

I miss you soft.
As soft as your breath against
The nape of my neck,
As soft as your lips against
The lobe of my ear.

I miss you.
That is all I do.
And I haven't even met you yet.

Finally. Tears.

My Spot

I'm not strong enough.
I thought I was
But, I'm not strong enough.

I sit on the same bench
In the park by the lake.
I can see my spot from here.
I should be sitting
In my spot — along the shore, under swaying branches
But, it hasn't been long enough.
Yet.

I showed it to you, once.
You liked it, you said.
You could see why I liked it, you said.
And, we kissed for the first time, there.
We did.

It was my spot.
Now, as my bare feet play
With grass and dandelions
I realize it is of no use.
I'll have to choose another

I'd Rather Not

Some days, I'd rather not think
Some days I'd rather not know
That it has been this long
That it is time to go.

Some days I need to hold on
A little while longer and then
Enough to make me believe
I'm strong enough to be.

I close my eyes real tight
And shut the darkness in
A comfort holds me close
I'm fine if I can't see.

Some days, I'd rather not think
Some days, I'd rather not see
But we don't always get what we want
Do we?

That Fall In Letchworth Park

Against cascading colours of yellow and
burnt orange and bright orange and
blazing red and wine red and
almost blue and other hues
With names as yet unknown
We held each other.

We talked to several strangers
Too happy to mind asking them
To take our photos
Preserving the memory of a perfect day.

I'd printed them. I wish I hadn't.
The pictures make me cry.
There we were, by the small oak burning red
Now or never, I thought then.
Through my smile I asked, "Could we?"
I held that smile — and my breath
But, nothing came
back
to
me.

The House Does Not Work

These rain drops are loud.
I can hear them from here.
Perhaps it's because
The hum of the dryer
Is their sole competition.

You do remember how much
I hate laundry's guts
Don't you?
You were kind enough to do it
Made no fuss and got right to it.
The trade-off was football.
It was all good.

Now, it's all very quiet.
Since you left
The house does not work.
It's empty,
lifeless
And cold.
And I endure the days as they drag on

Since you left.

That Thing You Did With Your Toes

Your voice makes me
Want to wake up next to you
Always has.
And, until another,
Perhaps always will.

I cannot put into words
How much I miss your touch
Your fingertips outlining my cheeks
Your caress up my thighs; my arms
Your cheek against my cheek
Then, you'd pull away a bit
Before gently placing your lips on mine.

I miss your kisses on my neck, my shoulders
My breasts
Tips aroused and inviting
Pulses in places hidden — good thing!
Beating out a pepper-seed rhythm of desire.

We honoured the divinity in each other.
Entering and beholding and exploring
Each other's temple.
You used every part of you to satisfy every part of me.
Oh for your kisses again
And that thing you did with your toes

Like Dying

Your words to me signalled an unbearable finality
I didn't want to hear them, but, I had to hear you out
I had to hear you say that this was, indeed, the end.
You did. And, it was.

The end of us
The end of us and we and our.
One call. Five minutes.
Years of heartache.

I grieved my loss in silence
I petted my sorrow in my bosom of discontent
What little words I found within and without
I used to mop up tears of anguish.
And, when the words were full
I'd wring them out again.

Nobody tells you it's like dying
I had heard you. Loud and clear. I was there.
But I felt better, safer, in denial.
My anger seethed and I drowned it in drink —
And ink — never to you.
I tried bargaining. I called. I wrote. You would have none.

How I got the courage to
Fulfill that pre-death obligation
Remains a mystery to me.
Fifty people at that party, and I'd never felt more alone.
On the way home — and at home — I cried.
What did you do? And how?
Me? I'm still working on accepting that we've died.

You Should Have Told Me

You should have told me
When you first decided to
Leave
You should have told me
When you first heard that little voice in your head
Telling you to go.

It's not fair that you had a heads-up
On our break-up
The decision to end us
Was not yours alone to make.

Please Call Me

I'm sitting by the phone
Waiting for it to ring
Waiting for you to call me
Call me! Dammit! Call me.

Why haven't you called?
Have you deleted my number?
You haven't deleted my number, have you?
Why have you deleted my number?

I have got to stop hearing ring tones
When there's none.
Rushing to answer texts that have not come in
In this and all the other ways
I hear from everyone but you
I don't want to hear from anyone *but* you.

Here comes another night
Another empty, lonely night
The pain gets worse when the lights go out
Please, please call me.

I Called Your Mom Today

I called your mom today
Hardly realized what I was doing
Until she picked up the phone.
I felt I needed to talk to her
To let her know that it was not my fault
But, I didn't go there.

It was a bit awkward, yes
But, not unbearable.
We had been friends, remember?
We'd spent so much time together.

I got through the pleasantries
The how are yous
The I'm fines
But then, I just wanted her to talk.

I don't know what I expected her to say
Only what I wanted her to say
Have longed to hear her say
From the time you'd said goodbye.

That you don't always make the best decisions
When it comes to matters of the heart
That you'd told her you'd made a mistake
But, she didn't go there.

I don't know what I was thinking
I hung up feeling as helpless as before
Emptiness birthed a crazy notion
So, I called your mom today.

She Could Have Been Ours

I was on the way to work this morning
When I heard a child cry
Her mother pushed the stroller to the side
Careful not to interrupt
The Bay Street flow
She paused to tend to her daughter.

I spotted them from several feet away
They had been headed in the opposite direction
I slowed my pace
No need to race
To a life more ordinary
Really.

As I came closer, I saw her face
A toddler — about two
She stopped me in my tracks
Her soft brown eyes held my gaze
Mixed — a little less me; more you.

Those few seconds were
The longest of my life
My heart picked up its pace, my eyes misted.
We would have made great parents
To a beautiful little girl.
I saw one today.
She looked like she could have been ours.

Some Days I Don't Miss You

Today I ran into a mutual friend
At least, he used to be
Since there's no us, then, there's no way
We have anything in common

He asked about you, just the same
Whether I had run into you
Whether I had heard from you
At all.

At first I was annoyed
Then, as he continued
I realized he was trying to make nice...

He changed the subject
To whether I still write and such
And, in the scorching lunch-time sun
We chatted about my project.

In case you're still interested:
It is a work-in-progress
And, of late, there's been more to do
It is easier to write when it's a good day
And some days I don't miss you.

It's Just Not Fair

If another chance at us were placed
On a silver platter
And all I would need to do is
Understand why
You are where you are, and
Why I am where I am.
I still would not be able to.
And I don't even care to understand!
After everything I was to you
Your rock, your help, your lover
It's just not fair.

If my life depended on
Connecting the dots,
If given an ultimatum to
Make sense of it all —
And live.
I would have to go with
My one, final, request.
A chance to whisper in everyone's ear
Asking them to explain to me
How it can be that you moved on
That you are now married — and, as I've heard, happily;
It's just not fair.

Shifting Moral of the Story

So smitten was I with the way
You moved me
In no time I let you in
In no time I was driven
To satisfy as you desired
And, so soon I became mired
In the mix of love and ugly
You were so deft to create.

Others who'd meant a lot to me
Grew distant
Which is to say, for me
They became summarily
Insufficient, compared to you
Your undivided attention was new
But, in time, grew thin
Scarce affections without and within.

By the time I awoke
You were gone.
Deserted — to cradle my new normal
To face the shifting moral
Of the story. Which one?
They all end in the same song
I gave up everything to make you stay
But you left, anyway.

The Power of Your Words

There are words I call your words
When I hear them, my pulse races
Beads of sweat decorate my hairline
And, for a long time
My mind plays them over and over
Trying to get used to them
Not the way you used them
To revile and hurt me.

Your words have come to have such power
They have lost their denotations
Only your meanings remain
Defined by context and time —
Like wine stain on a lovely dress —
And the measure of the pain
You caused when you first uttered them
It is time to disempower them
And set their true meanings free.

Out of This World

Of late I've been wondering
Whether, for all the time
We were together,
I was the other girl.
It might sound silly but
How else could I explain
The swiftness and the ease
With which you moved into
Another
girl.

I also have been wondering
Whether you had meant it
When you'd said
"You are, easily, my world."
How hard was it for you
To enter this new realm
Adapting to new cosmos
Out of this world but within
Another
girl?

Just Friends

Maybe you hadn't noticed
But the way you treated me
Set the standard for the way
She treated me.
You said you two were
Friends for years
Just friends.
For years.
And, I believed you.

But, the day came when
She whisked by me
Without so much as a nod
She went straight to your room
To talk, you'd said after
A space that belonged to
Just friends. Of many years.
I could hardly believe that.

Would she have treated me
With such disdain
Had you not been okay with it?
How did you speak to her about me?
She took her cue from you, dear one
She saw me through your eyes
Your old friend. Of many years.
I could not compete with that.

I Miss That

Remember when we took that picture
The one where I sat on your lap?
I hadn't wrapped my arms around you
I think because we were still new,
And I didn't want to come across as
Too strong.
But, it was an opportunity to show you
How much I cared about you even then,
And I missed that.

We were on a friend's patio, remember?
They'd invited us over for dinner
I didn't know how much you had told them
Our small display of affection?
Too much.
But, I should have turned and held you
Under the starred sky, waves lapping
I see that.

Over the next several months
We held each other over and over
Sometimes, close and in the company of others
Sometimes, just brushed as we walked by each other
This much.
Maybe I should have held you tighter
Your scent, your smile, your touch, all gone
I miss that.

Nothing That Mattered

It is Sunday night
And I have work tomorrow
Do you know what I did
All weekend long?
Nothing — that mattered.

It was beautiful out
I could see it from the living room
Sunny, leaves shivered
But, ever so gently
I imagine it was beautiful out.

I did not leave the house
There was no point
I could not think of anywhere
I simply had to be
Of anyone who simply needed me.

No, I needed me
I needed me to be present
Function in the moment
But, for two whole days
I did nothing — that mattered.

Out of Time

Nothing excites me anymore
Nothing says Bam! or Zowie!
Nothing new. Same church, different pew.
No Boom Shaka Laka
Around here.

Here, Lonely. Alone.
I am yearning for my him.
And God doesn't seem to hear.
Here I am.
But barely.

Incomplete. Unfulfilled. Drained .
My life sucked out
My life sucks
My life is sucking the life
Out of misery and despair.

Out of touch
Out of sync
Out of care
Out of time.

Other Than Myself

All my days are filled with staring
Through my window
Gazing at the concrete jungle
And people going nowhere that important

Occasionally I visit with online people
Or so they say they are
It's a place to go
And I go there
To get away from here
And my mind.

I would like to get away
Fly far away
Soar to my heart's content
Then make a beeline for my bed
And sink between the pillows.
Have no one ask where I am
Or how I am
Or, even if they do,
I do not answer
Because I do not have to.

And when it gets too hot
Between the pillows and
Under the sheets
I drag myself downstairs
To visit with the dogs.
Make them make me get excited
Get cracking on caring about something
Other than myself and nothing.

An Image of You

I have said quite a lot to you
Over the past few days
None within earshot, of course
All in my mind.
To the image of you in my mind.
And heart.
Yes, there's an image of you
Engraved on my heart.

I wish I had the courage to say
What's really on my mind
I have the right words, the right sighs
All lined up.
With this image that I have of you
Inside.
But, too late. The picture
No longer reflects reality.

Nothing

Sometimes I sit and stare at nothing
And nothing stares back.
Nothing can help me with this hurt
I carry in my heart, my mind, my spirit
Nothing says this is just a dream
A horrible dream that will soon end
Nothing stares back at me.

Nothing listens to the sound of my tears
Falling on my pillow both morning and night
Making their way through the fibres
Until they can run no more
Trapped in an endless weave of
An unfamiliar maze
Nothing knows how that feels.

You left me with nothing
I have the scent of the pillow next to mine
And nothing smells like it.
Your sweet body mixed with shampoo
I can almost taste it
As I can almost taste your kiss
And nothing tastes quite like it.

I Just Don't Feel Like It

I don't feel like thinking about you tonight
I don't feel like arguing with the imaginary you
Giving witty comebacks to the reasons you give
When I ask why you're leaving.

I don't feel like smiling at the good memories
I don't feel like getting angry
I just don't feel like doing anything tonight
Except finishing this tub of ice-cream.

A Moving Target

You said there would be other times
Even as you said goodbye
You promised that you would never
Be too far away.
Even though I could not make you stay
— Believe me, I tried —
You said I shouldn't worry
That both our futures held moments
When we would be together
Even if not in the same way.

I was blinded by hurt and confusion
What else could I have done
But believe you because I wanted to
Had to — desperately — believe
Even as I clung to
What I knew could not
Would not be true
Still, just to hear you say it
Gave me something to look forward to
In the end, it was just a moving target.

Sometimes There Are No Thoughts of You

Sometimes there are no thoughts
Of you.
I find myself at a loss
For words, or sounds
Or a smell or a sight
Anything!
Just, anything that says
You were here
And you meant
Everything to me.

Sometimes I can't quite remember
Your words.
My mind gets mixed up
With what you really said
And what I wished you had said
Blurred!
My thoughts, your words
My vision of how we were
Maybe we were not as lovely
As I had thought.

The Nights Have All Been Spent

Today was my last day with you
You didn't know it but
I've been counting down
The days on the calendar
How much longer
I would let you linger
Hold you in my heart
Play with you in my mind

Tonight was my last night with you
Holding pillows that
Took your place
As I embraced your memory.
It hasn't been easy
But the nights have all been spent
And tomorrow, I start again.

Without the Kill

The nape of my neck is all aflame
As the sun's rays beat down
Mercilessly.
The hem of my blouse flutters
Responding to the whiff of breeze
That takes the slightest edge
Off the heat.

I am wrapped in a heat
That cannot be ignored.
Too tightly wound, I am
Unable to move.

Hot and breezy
Trapped. Uneasy.
Like the way you have me going
Friend to lover
Bi-lovely.

It's how you make me feel hope
Yet hopeless
How you hold me
But without caress
How you kiss me. Hard.
Without the kill.
And, kill me softly
Without the will
To love me
Back to life.

Not Again

Not again
Because
You are not as beautiful
As I once thought you to be.
You are not as beautiful
As a day without
A memory of you.

You Can't Make This Love Up

I hope when true love blindsides you, it will find you in the best of health — emotional health, mental health and a healthy approach to life.

There is no fear in love.

Be happy.

Be glad for those who are genuinely happy for you. Be understanding of those who are not. Be thankful you're able to tell them apart.

Have you waited so long, when true love finally arrives (that day when your ship comes in and you're not at the airport) you're almost afraid to touch it, much less embrace and enjoy it? Touch it. Embrace it. Enjoy it. You'll think if you squeeze it too tightly, it might break. You can't break this love up.

You may catch yourself thinking that, at some point, you're gonna do something stupid; that it's only a matter of time. Ever get that? Stop thinking. Stop over-thinking. You are who you are and how you are. You have been, and are being, true to yourself. You are the you with whom he/she has fallen in love. All your persnicketyness and what-nots have been duly accounted for.

Finally, someone who also turns the hangers facing in. Honey? You can't mess this love up.

Have you heard the one about not wanting to go to sleep because reality is now better than your dreams? Now you'll know what the heck they were talking about. (Brownie points if you now wake up smiling. Uh-huh.)

Oh! And the one about when you finally meet the one, you'll understand why it never worked out with anyone else? It will finally make perfect sense as the pieces fall into place.

Oh! Oh! And the one about there being someone, somewhere, who's wondering what it would be like to meet someone like you? Well, honey, they are about to find out!

Whaddya know? Those who cared about you were right all along. You'll find it's effortless and beautiful. You can't make this love up.

And, when he/she tells you, you are perfect, just smile knowingly and say, "No, we're just right for each other."

You will remember the adage: "If a relationship has to be a secret, you should not be in it." And, you will be glad you took heed.

Vulnerability. Yeeeaah. About that. Here's the thing: Can you trust that person with yours? And, as they learn your imperfections, do they love you anyway? Yes? Then, beyond the jones, you've got a good thing going on.

Does being with him/her inspire you to be a better human being?

Is the default set to repair or replace?

What of your core beliefs and values? Hey, "Opposites attract but likes stay together."

Have the difficult conversations. You must.

Play.

No games.

Have at least one song that no one else in the world knows you both listen and dance to. Together.

Have a "This is our song!" song you can dance to — or not — in public.

The whole of your happiness together should be greater than the sum of each happiness apart.

My Marlena. Of all the sentiments expressed in that love story *Water for Elephants*, that's all I remember. My Marlena. Whose *my* will I be? (Sit still my daughter, until thou know how the matter will fall.) Heh heh.

The heart of her husband doth safely trust in her, so that he shall have no need of spoil. She will do him good and not evil all the days of her life. (Proverbs 31:11-12) Love the way that's put.

God is holding your heart. And He has promised to restore to you the years that the locusts have eaten.

Behold His Something New! It is indeed Something Beautiful and Something Far Better. And, yet, would you be willing to give it all up for Him? Yes? Know that He honours and rewards that faith.

Stand still.

Sit still.

Be still.

Kiss with your eyes closed. Always. And, when you do, nothing else in the world should matter — at all.

Make love with wild abandon as you honour the divinity in each other.

Love thickly. Don't be afraid of being loved thickly in return.

Didn't see that coming, did you?

Me neither.

***

PHASE THREE
— I DID NOT SEE THIS COMING —

Open Your Eyes And Love Me

When we make love
I want you to be aware of me
I want you to be aware of me
Loving you
Needing you. More.

Open your eyes
And look at me feeling you
Touching you.
Close your eyes and
Sense me
All over your body
See me with your mind's eye
Taking all of you
As much as all of me
Will allow.

And, as you feel me feeling you
And feeling for you
As you sense me being aroused
By your sensuality
As you see me taking you
Open your lips
And love me.

I'm Always Thirsty After Poetry

I'm always thirsty after poetry
So very thirsty
As if there's a space inside me
That needs, desperately,
To be filled
With a tall order
Of a satisfying drink.

Each poem takes away
A little piece of clothing
As each seeks to get closer home.
Each wanting to embed itself
Nearest to my heart.

I am soon naked
Naked. And hot.
And so very thirsty
Thirsting for that which will quench me
Thoroughly.

Sand In My Shorts

You took me from my dream
Into your reality
Everything I had ever hoped for
You handed to me
Under a star-spangled platter
Then, nothing else seemed to matter
But you're sharing my fantasy
That dream you had now realized.

And, in your eyes
I saw you doubting
Whether all of this was real
And I closed my eyes
And consumed you
While I had sand
In the folds of my shorts.

Company

My most beautiful moments
Have been with you
Under a black velvet sky
By the sea —
You, my dreams and me.

With your laughter
You share the music of my heart
The rhythms of my soul
All that I've longed for
To have and to hold.

On to your thoughts
That you share with me
You touch. I feel.
There's more to meeting
Than just company.

My most beautiful moments
Sharing our laughter, our thoughts
With the wind
By the sea
You, our dreams, and me.

Bayou

'Twas best to take a walk
Along the tranquil shores
Each footstep imprinted
On the cold hard sand
And, with a wave of her hand
Half purpose, half despair
She closes her eyes
And straightens her hair.

Here, in the wide open
Free and breezy atmosphere
Who cares if a lock or two
Is out of place?
If her deepest thoughts
Are on her face.

Alone at night
A moonlit night
As breezes lift her frock
Above her waist.
It is time to take a rest.

In the beauty of her nakedness
Her mind is set at ease
And now with each piece of
Fire dancing on the water
The bayou
Sings of Mayou
And her "certainty of tides."

With Every Other Step

It's been such a long time
I have almost forgotten how
But I simply had to write
Because I have reason to, now.

How absolutely thrilling
And wonderful and nice
Your actions were toward me
Underneath the starry skies.

How effortlessly you moved me
You wooed me and you gave
All that I had been longing for
Even more than I had craved.

For how could I have known
You could make me feel so wanted
So special in the ways and times
Your lips remained undaunted.

The how you kissed. The when you kissed
With every other step I knew
I should have been kissed a long time
Before now — by you.

Time and Company

You tell me that you want
My time and company
Should I take it then
That you want me?

There's not much more to me
When you take those away
Is it that you're telling me
You want me to stay

With you for the rest of my life?
Now, just look at that, shall we?
It would appear you've read my mind
Again. You make it seem easy.

Funny though you feel that way
May I share this with you?
Time and company are fine
But, my love, I want you, too.

Naked

My wall broke this morning
My prison of supposed defence
My fortress of fear
Came down. Block by block.

And I — I stood bare.
Naked.
For a moment, held my breath
Then, nothing happened
It dawned on me
That nothing would happen.
I exhaled.

And, as the smile came to my lips
I realized that I no longer
Had to cringe at the thought
Of having my heart
Eroded
If you came too close.

I smiled
And when I spoke
At that moment I broke
Into laughter.

For I realized
As the words fell
I was now free.
It was okay for me
To be. Just be.

Just For A Moment

Just for a moment
Can you take a moment
To listen to me?

I want to tell you
How I feel about you
In a way that it has
Never been said before.
But, to heck with originality
There is so much more.

 I love you.
That's it.
I love you.
I find you warm, lovable, sensible, kind and loving.
With all that you are
I want to make a life with you
I want to make a love with you
A very special love.
It mightn't be original
But it will be special
Because it will be ours
Created by our hearts
Shaped by our hands.

Understand?
With all its imperfections
With all its moments of uncertainty
Over what seemed an eternity
With all its moments of doubts and fears
And, too, with all its tears.

Tears because there is so much joy
So much you. So much me.
Because we have given of ourselves to each other
So many beautiful moments and memories.

Just for a moment
Listen to me saying
I love you.

How Do You Know?

Is your hidden camera
Pinned next to the heart
On my sleeve?
Your words on point
They don't disappoint
Moving me in ways
You would not believe.

Air

Locked inside the
passion of
Kama Sutra
His touch is air
I breathe
Deeply

He moves
Me
In places
Still reserved

Until

In incriminating surrender
I lose all inhibition.
I am his.

Epiphany

I hear the distance I travel
I feel the distance I fear
Spanning the height
Between ground and endless sky
My feet are off the ground
And I am high.

This is neither flying
Nor soaring. An epiphany.
I'm being transported into
A vast nothingness
Losing all sense of context
And motion and time and space
I feel the distance increasing
I go up, up, and away.

Hands over ears
I melt inside
No tears
Can't cry if I can't feel
Now, can I?
Am I there yet?
No, higher yet.

Soon, I morph into a shadow
Of my former self
Looming evanescent
Still.
Nothing happens.
Suddenly
My thoughts are crystal clear.

This moving, my doing
This distance, my desire.
Is my fear of heights weaker
Than my fear of loving you?
Than I fear being loved by you?

I was prepared to die flying
Than I was to die trying
At something new with you.
Something ethereal, yet true.

I don't have a fear of heights
I have a fear of falling.
I have a fear of loving
And falling into you.

Your Kisses

Your kisses are rain drops
Here comes another shower
Refreshing and new
I want to be drenched
Soaked right through.

But each rain drop is filled
With its own flame
Fires of desire
Engrave my name
Upon your tongue, your passion
Your unwavering attention.

Your rain-fire kisses
Wash and renew me
Delight and destroy me
Thoroughly consume me.

Requited Love

Now when these words
Leave my lips
I am not afraid
They will fall on ears
That would rather not hear them
On a heart
That would rather not feel them
Make their impression
On a mind
That would rather dismiss them
Because the love of my heart
Does not reciprocate them.

Now when these words
Leave my lips
They do not carry the burden
Nor the audacity
Of hope.
They do not need to wish for
A welcoming heart and mind.

Now when these words
Leave my lips
I know
For sure
They leave me
Unfettered.
I am left relieved
As they take a certain flight
To your heart and mind
Waiting.
Welcoming.
Reciprocating.

Closer

You are next to me
On your side of the bed
You slip your hand across
My waist.
You pull me to you.
Closer.
I smile, "I can't get any closer, my love."
You close your eyes and inhale me.
Closer still.
"I want you under my skin."

Rush of Love

You're loving me so fast
I can't write fast enough.
I wake up covered in
The scent and flavour of you.
Your kisses tell me you're here for this
Your embrace says I am yours.
We arouse each other's minds
Our hearts are in sync
To think
This is really happening.

Back to Life

I thought I had
No more strength or time for love
Until you came
I made the time
You gave me strength.

I wanted more of you
Wanting me
You said I gave you hope
By just being me.

In your eyes I see
How you take pleasure
In pleasing me
My love, no need to fear
Losing me at all.

For the first time
No second thoughts
Your strong arms
And long kisses
Comforted me home.

Your words wooed me
Your actions moved me
Into the new me
As you loved me
Back to life.

About the Author

Claudia Williams has been writing — journal entries, poems, short stories, novellas — since her early teens. At Fortyish, she finally found the courage to publish this part of herself told in poetry over decades. For those who are able to relate, she hopes this anthology will be like a hand to hold. She has done many public readings of her poems to receptive audiences and much acclaim. Claudia is Jamaican-Canadian, and lives in Ontario, Canada. She has a website, www.cyopro.com (Create Your Own Productions), and she can also be found on Twitter @cyopro. Claudia is a regular host of her niece's favourite: Girls' Night!

www.ingramcontent.com/pod-product-compliance
Lightning Source LLC
Chambersburg PA
CBHW070111080526
44586CB00013B/1265